WHAT YOU
SHOULD KNOW
ABOUT

SELLING AND
SALESMANSHIP

By MILTON B. BURSTEIN

1969
OCEANA PUBLICATIONS, INC.
DOBBS FERRY, NEW YORK

Number 18 in the
BUSINESS ALMANAC SERIES

*Each volume in the Business Almanac Series
is designed to introduce you to an aspect of
modern American Business theory and practice.*

DEDICATION

This book is dedicated to those young men and women who are anticipating a career in sales, to those men and women in sales who have the innate ability and drive but need a new set of rules and guide lines to achieve new heights, and to those employers who would aid their sales force in setting these guide lines.

This book is also dedicated to my daughter, Enid, whose pride in her dad has helped keep alive that determination to excel in all endeavors including sales.

TABLE OF CONTENTS

Page

ABOUT THE AUTHOR

Milt Burstein has successfully run the gamut in selling. Retail sales while a University student were followed by all other forms of marketing and selling.

Initially employed as a salesman in the garment industry, he progressed to sales manager and ultimately became a partner in a manufacturing firm. Leaving the apparel field for the country's money markets, Mr. Burstein started as a salesman of investment securities and mutual funds and became successively vice president and president of brokerage firms specializing in the sale of New Issues of Stocks and of Mutual Funds. He also negotiated acquisitions and sales of companies.

Other successes in salesmanship have included the position of National Director of a sales division of the country's largest land developer. Mr. Burstein also set up and managed a European division, selling Florida land to European Nationals.

Working for subsidiaries of the same parent company, he set records in various franchise sales and conducted sales training classes and sales seminars.

For relaxation, Mr. Burstein is a golf course duffer, an amateur magician, and an excellent comic and story teller. He has performed frequently at veterans hospitals and for charitable organizations.

PREFACE

This book is one that had to be written. At various plateaus in selling, a search of libraries for sources of information, failed to offer this author many of the inside details necessary to achieve success more rapidly.

All books on selling seemed to be limited in scope to a pure text approach without offering tips and answers to problems from a more practical viewpoint. This does not infer that many of the books studied, at the time, were not valuable for the student and neophyte salesman. Many of them were excellent for gaining an insight to sales with multitudinous samples and examples of various steps in the making of a sale.

However, no book, uncovered during this period, offered the combination of being a training text book for the student, a source of additional information, learned and offered in a practical manner for the salesman who is trying to upgrade and increase his earnings, and also a reference book for the business man who wants a deeper insight into the sales function of his business. Hence this volume is the result of knowledge accrued over a period of successful selling and recruiting and training of salesmen.

Several factors had to be taken into account to produce the book envisaged. First, keep it short. A lengthy verbose tome would defeat its own purpose. Second, cover all phases of the sale fully so that they can be understood and used at all levels. Third, offer in detail that extraneous information necessary to successful selling that may not be as fully available elsewhere.

I believe these aims have been fully covered and anyone who knows this book has an excellent head start.

Information that is not readily available elsewhere, but, can prove extremely valuable is included in all of the chapters. However, some of the highlights of this are included in the chapter on prospecting where additional sources of potential customers and potential business are fully outlined. Again in the chapter on itineraries, the information has been amassed during a period of intensive travel that brought the author honorary membership in many of the special air lines clubs that existed at the time. Clubs such as United Air Lines Half Million Miler; American Air Lines Admiral; Pan American's Clipper Club; Delta Air Line's Flying Colonels and National Air Line's Three Coast Club. Proper usage of the information in this chapter can save thousands of dollars and hundreds of hours of time.

One other chapter that offers information that has not been covered in any of the available books found but is constantly increasing in importance with today's marketing trends is the chapter on franchising.

The balance of the book, combined with these highlighted here, will, I know, supply all of the information necessary for success.

1

SELLING AND SALESMANSHIP

"Nothing Happens Until Somebody Sells Something"

The above quote has been with us for many years and has been used by sales managers and trainers in seminars, lectures, recruiting programs, etc. for almost as many years. The source of this quote is lost in oblivion, but the essence is more true each year.

We are all of us constantly selling during the entire course of our lives. This includes the man who professes to dislike selling as well as the so called "born salesman."

The child who utilizes cute ways or tears to achieve an action or result from his or her parent is selling, the swain who convinces the girl to accept his proposal of marriage has sold himself and conversely, the girl who induces her boy friend to propose has sold herself. But these examples are nowhere near the sum total of our constant selling. For example, when a husband attempts to convince his wife that he should go to the ball game, lodge meeting, or poker game because the relaxation or contacts will result in many advantages, either material or intangible, he is selling. In the same context, the wife who wants a new or more expensive fur coat embarks on a selling campaign to convince her husband of the advantages entailed in the purchase.

Not only in our personal lives but in our normal business relationships we must sell ourselves to our co-workers to insure cooperation, we must sell ourselves and our

1

abilities to our superiors to achieve greater degrees of success as evinced in promotions and increased income. In our social contacts, we must sell ourselves as desireable people to know in order to make friends.

In short, we never stop selling. In our personal and our family lives, in our business lives, in our social lives, we are constantly selling to achieve results and goals.

Salesmanship, however, takes the every day selling and elevates it to the professional category.

Many definitions of salesmanship have been offered by as many authorities in the field. They all boil down in essence to two basic meanings:

1. Salesmanship is the technique and methods used to sell goods or ideas successfully.

2. Salesmanship is the ability to successfully sell goods and ideas.

Put simply, salesmanship is an ability and a technique. The professional salesman is constantly working to improve his technique and increase his ability, because therein lies increased income and of equal importance to the good salesman, personal satisfaction.

The professional salesman who can move merchandise or services is the man who keeps the plant running and the production and administrative people employed. Just as the salesman must have the product to sell, no manufacturing, billing, supervising, etc. can or would be done if no markets were created for the product.

That salesman who knows his profession and all aspects of selling is the professional salesman. The highest accolade that can be given a real salesman is to call him a "pro." This statement by his peers and employers is the equivalent, in the selling field, to the Oscar Award in the entertainment field.

This book will deal with the basic facts and know-how in the making of a professional salesman, the various steps entailed in the making of a sale and techniques to best accomplish the final sale.

Although the techniques here are tried and proven, they are in no means limited to those that will be portrayed. There is no field or profession that is as broad in scope, as unconfined and unrestricted in operation as professional salesmanship. In addition, the personal satisfaction and feeling of accomplishment, as well as earnings potential, are as rewarding as any man could desire. The only limitations are your own desire and willingness to work.

The amount of application and effort put into salesmanship will show themselves in the results and earnings of the salesman. An oft quoted, and true, statement of the profession is "20% of the salesman do 80% of the volume and conversely 80% of the salesmen do 20% of the volume." Basically, the top 20% are the "pros", the men who know and work their craft best. You too can join this inner circle.

General Headings Of Types Of Salesmanship

Salesmanship will vary with the type of merchandise sold, type of firm represented, and type of markets available. The selling steps of prospecting, approach, presentation or demonstration, and close will be greatly effected by these variations.

The salesman who sells to a professional buyer or merchant for resale must rarely create a need for the basic product. The salesmanship technique here is to demonstrate, that of all similar products, his product is of the best quality, styling, or price, and the purchase of this product offers the best profit opportunities.

In the same sense, the insurance or mutual fund salesman must frequently convince his customer that he has a need for his product in the first place.

3

To the door to door salesman selling cheap gadgets, anyone who answers a knock on the door is a prospect. The highly technical sales engineer, however, may find his prospecting and potential markets limited to those few companies that can use and afford a highly sophisticated and very expensive piece of special equipment.

Other factors which will have an important control of a salesman's scope, are the differentiation between products such as staples, style merchandise and specialty merchandise. Also brand names that have a pre-created desire would be marketed in a different fashion than the products of a little known manufacturer.

Although this book will not attempt to answer all questions for all salesmen, it will set proven guide lines adaptable to all. Your own ingenuity will show you how to utilize them.

The following is a simple chart indicating the principle type of salesmen and markets:

TYPES OF SALESMEN AND MARKETS

Employer	Primary Markets Sold	Principal Customer Types	Type of Salesman
Manufacturer or Service Co.	Wholesaler Jobber Retailer Industrial user	Professional Buyer Purchasing Agent	Field Salesman Store or Showroom Salesman
Wholesaler or Jobber	Retailer or Industrial user	Professional Buyer Purchasing Agent	Field Salesman Store or Showroom Salesman

Retailer or Service Co.	Consumer	Walk-in customer looking to buy The prospect to be converted	Counter Clerk Dept. Salesman Inside and outside salesman Direct creative salesman
Technical Manufacturer or Service Co.	Industrial user	Purchasing agent Engineer Plant Head	Sales Engineer Serviceman Salesman

2

PROSPECTING

A salesman who has no one to tell about his wares must perforce be unsuccessful. This is patently true even if his product is the best, his knowledge most complete, and his personality most winning. Hence the first step in successful salesmanship is the locating of prospects or prospecting.

Definition Of Prospects And Prospecting

A Prospect is anyone who can reasonably use the product or service being offered and, equally as important, can afford to pay for it. One other consideration that might limit this description is the willingness of the seller to sell to the specific prospect. This limitation is predicated on the possibility of an unusual nature of the product, or exclusivity, or character of potential purchaser. An example of this limitation could be the refusal of an exclusive club to sell a membership to a known criminal.

Prospecting is a form of exploration. Prospecting is the seeking out and finding of people who meet the requirements of being a prospect.

For many years the term suspect was also used. This was supposedly someone who might or might not develop into a prospect. In other words, anyone at all.

This author and many other sales managers and sales trainers have found that the suspect terminology resulted in lost prospects, wasted time, and accomplished no purpose. Briefly, if there is a chance he can or will buy, he is a prospect unless follow up qualifications prove otherwise.

Prospecting By Types Of Sales Operations

Differences in type of sales, type of product, type of market and type of industry can have a tremendous effect on the amount and nature of prospecting necessary for the salesman.

For example at the retail level, both the clerk and top notch retail store salesman, have very little occasion to seek out customers. In most cases they wait on their "next" as he comes into the store. Repeat customers may ask for their specific favorite salesman, thereby advancing his "next." These customers were brought in by store location, window displays, and advertising.

However, notice the words "very little occasion," the pro at this level can, with imagination, increase his scope. A smart clothing salesman will keep a record of all of his personal customers and their preferences and sizes. As he gets to know them, he will send them advance personal notice of special sales or events, the arrival of new merchandise that might interest them, etc. With this type of base, and subtle suggestion, he can frequently get them to bring or send friends in, thereby building a much larger fund of personal customers.

The retail salesman who works in and out of the store has a much great latitude and opportunity to increase his prospects. The periods when he is not on call for the next customer should not be spent gabbing with the boys or playing gin.

If the average real estate salesman wishes to become a member of the top 20%, this time can be utilized contacting new or expanding industries to get the names of people to be relocated into the area, canvassing desireable neighborhoods for new listings, sending mailings, etc. In the same manner, the auto showroom salesman can be out putting cards on windshields that offer special trade-in deals, contacting people with ailing vehicles, potential fleet users, and new licensees. The same possibilities exist in all industries.

The necessity, up and down the line, is a willingness to work, and a vivid imagination. An outstanding example of this is the travel wholesaler who originated the idea of merchandising tours in super markets and in mail order catalogues.

In other areas of selling, the wholesaler or jobber sells to retailers or industrial users, and the manufacturer sells to wholesalers, jobbers, retailers, and industrial users. In most cases there are store or show room salesmen who just service the customers who walk in and field salesmen who call only on accounts in a territory.

The average salesman, covering the territory, limits himself to existing accounts and to those in the same field as his present market. These names for this prospecting can usually be found in classified telephone directories and in special books or lists that are compiled and sold within an industry. This is a form of prospecting that is commendable but, by its nature, very limited. The real pro finds other markets and other outlets. There are many evident results of professional sales thinking at this level.

For years greeting cards were sold in card and stationery stores. The first sales prospector with imagination put them into drug stores also, and today you almost always see racks of greeting cards in lobbies of motels. Can you envisage the tremendous new market and new supply of prospects this approach created?

Another example is the taking small apparel items from the shelves of department stores and specialty stores and successfully merchandising them from super market racks.

There are two other categories of salesmen that fit into

the above grouping. The special skill salesman such as the sales engineer, and the serviceman salesman. These also work in limited markets, but a true knowledge and analysis of their product or service may offer many clues to broader markets, more prospects, and increased earnings.

The final group under discussion in this category is the direct to consumer salesman. This is the group that encounters the highest degree of sales resistance. Whether the item is tangible or intangible, a high ticket item or an inexpensive bauble, their task is more difficult but usually their remuneration more satisfactory. Door to door canvasses are not included in this group.

Unlike the salesmen mentioned in the above instances, these direct salesmen do not sell to professional buyers, professional purchasing agents, or people who have walked in to buy. Their approach is usually to the cold lead who does not even know, at first contact, that he wants, or has use for the product or service being offered. This category does not consist of only the home sales expert but can also include the selling of a new concept to industry. An example of this was the Electronic Data Processing salesman a few short years ago.

In the case of the professional buyer or purchasing agent, the buying motivation is obvious. In creative sales, it is frequently hidden, or must be created.

In the next paragraphs we will outline the more important principals and methods of prospecting for leads. Most of these will apply to the direct or creative salesman because the nature of his work offers a much wider latitude and much greater continuing necessity for this function.

Principals and Methods of Lead Prospecting

The basic principal of lead prospecting entails finding the person who meets the requirements of being a prospect. Of basic importance in this function is qualifying this lead, to the best of your ability, to determine if the need and desire exist or can be created and if the potential prospect can afford to pay for the product or services offered. Good judgment is an all important factor because time is one of the salesman's most valuable assets.

The salesman who is more efficient at qualifying leads will, naturally, waste less time making pointless presentations. However, the tendency to make a fetish of qualifying these prospects, must also be avoided. Some salesmen spend so much time qualifying their leads, they allow themselves very little time to sell. A natural and intelligent balance must be maintained.

The salesman who properly organizes himself and establishes good working habits in prospecting, and good judgement in qualifying, will make a greater number of productive presentations to interested and qualified prospects. Hence, the opportunity for more closes and more success will be present.

Excellent tools for prospecting are lined canary yellow legal size pads and 3x5 file cards. An easy way to work is to make all suggested lists on the pad and, after initial contact, if there is occasion to follow up, transpose the information to the file card. The cards can then be tabbed or filed by date of follow up, or they can be filed geographically for convenience of follow up.

Listed below are some of the best methods for securing the names you need. As you progress in sales others will occur to you.

1. Personal contact list: This is primarily for the direct salesman. This list should take several weeks to compile. First list your close friends and relatives, those in your address book, etc. Next start to put down the names of acquaintances. If you do not know the name for sure, make a note that will

recall him to mind and follow up at a future date. The merchants you do business with, i.e. your grocer; his employees; your tailor; his employees; your clothier; his employees; your luncheonette, etc. This group should also include servicemen such as your T.V. repair; your service station and the like. The members of your church and other religious affiliations; the members of your fraternal groups; service and other organizations (frequently this list is available from the group). Your business associates; past and present co-workers; employers or employees; your neighbors and people who share hobbies, vacations or other forms of recreation with you, should be included. When this list is completed, its size will astound you. The average man knows over four hundred people when he lists them all. All of these are prospects for a direct sale.

2. Referrals: This is for all levels of salesmen. The direct salesman can usually convince each name on the list to give him over five additional names to bring his list to over two thousand. Each of these, in turn, will radiate up to five more to create an ever increasing list of prospects. The wholesale salesman may get entree into only one or two new accounts by referrals from existing accounts but the main point is to ASK FOR THE REFERRAL.

3. Newspaper items: Items indicating promotions in job, personnel changes, changes in industries or locations, new stores, births, deaths, and marriage notices, real estate sales or purchases, golden age doings, are useful information for the sale of many varied commodities and services.

4. Public records: Records showing all of the details listed in number 3 plus new corporations registration, new licenses to drive, to engage in business, to build, and to do anything else will indicate markets.

5. Arrival of buyers notices in newspapers: The use of these is restricted but obvious.

11

6. Distribution of hand bills: This can be done through hand distribution, Take-one stands, under door placement, bag stuffing in super markets, etc.

7. Mail order advertising with return coupon: This can be done to purchased lists of individual types of prospects, to individual industries from the yellow pages, town directories to controlled income areas, and various other means of list accumulation. This can also include cooperative mailing with local merchants.

8. Newspaper advertising: Coupon type ads to get interested prospects to write to you. This can be in major publications, or local shopper, or penny saver newspapers.

9. Telephone sales: There are items and services that can be sold on the phone. However, in most cases, the phone is a much more useful instrument for securing appointments. A good catchy phone presentation should be developed. If calling a referral on the phone, the full name of the referring party, first and last name, should be mentioned. "Bill Jones suggested I call you." When asking for an appointment, be specific, do not say "When can I see you?" Rather, say "Is Tuesday at 4:00 P.M. convenient?" This method of establishing the appointment is much more effective. One important point—keep it brief, give a minimum of information and ask for the appointment.

10. Work with other sales people: Do not work with people with shady or unscrupulous reputations, and do not work with direct competitors. However, other reputable salesmen selling to the same type of accounts will usually cooperate with you to help you gain entree to their accounts if you will reciprocate.

11. Give gifts or pay cash for names of prospects: Print listing sheets for names and on the sheet offer some form of reward for either the names or for consummated sales.

12. Offer gifts for interviews: Circularize your lists and make a special offer to anyone who will give your salesman (yourself) one hour of their time to hear about your wonderful offer.

13. Find people with special interests: These can constitute a whole new market. One security salesman built one of the most successful customer lists in this manner. He had a report made on the stock and operations of a manufacturer of electronic testing devices. This was followed by phone calls to standards engineers in the area. The conversation started with discussion of the product line and testing devices, at which point he mentioned that he was a securities broker and had a report he would send without obligation. Follow-up phone calls produced customers in 12% of the cases. The same broker used a stock report on a proprietary pharmaceutical manufacturer to phone druggists. The same amount of original thinking can be applied to many other fields.

14. Purchase lists: In most fields that have professional buyers or purchasing agents, lists are published and can be purchased. In the case of consumer sales, selection of type of lists would require much more thought.

15. Analyze and list potential users: This is a list for all forms of sales. List all of the types of users that you currently include in your customer or prospect list. Then analyze your product or service and think of who else could use these. In some cases, a different approach or presentation might be necessary. But, as in the examples shown earlier in this chapter, enough thought can produce tremendous new markets and outlets.

16. Company leads: These are the gravy, and consist of leads developed through the various marketing programs used by the company.

17. Visual inspection or intuition: Frequently visual signs will indicate a need for your program. A

broken down car will tell an auto salesman something as will a rotting house siding speak to a
home improvement man. However, sometimes the
signal is much more subtle, and the potentiality
of the prospect is sensed in a more intuitive fashion.
18. Hire canvassers or phone workers: Give them a for-
mat and pay them to make appointments for you.

The various lead-getting methods mentioned here can
be enlarged and enhanced by the thinking salesman. However, use of just some of these can insure prospecting
success. In many cases, a first glance might indicate that
many of these methods are not applicable in your field
of salesmanship. Do not pass them by with this first
glance. Restudy of most of these methods and the use of
some variations could open up a completely new set of
horizons and new worlds to conquer.

3

THE APPROACH

There is a desparity of opinions in the sales profession as to what point in the over all sale constitutes the approach. There are as many alternate ideas as there are authorities. Some feel that the first contact either by phone or by mail is the approach to the customer. Others will say only phone conversations make up an approach.

In the opinion of this author and many authoritative sources, all of the above are part of prospecting. In fact all steps from the determining of whom are prospects until the personal meeting, when the sale is attempted, fall under the heading of prospecting.

The actual approach is the physical confrontation between salesman and prospect. It is that point when his appearance, demeanor, and what he says will determine if he will have an opportunity to make an adequate presentation.

As in all of the other steps that compromise a successful sale, the approach can frequently predetermine whether or not a salesman can show his wares and whether or not he will receive proper attention. Good approaches are an important ingredient of salesmanship and are not difficult to develop.

Background Information About Customer

There is a certain amount of preliminary work that must be accomplished before the approach is made. This work will vary greatly between different types of sales and products. But, whether to a greater or lesser degree, some of it should be accomplished to succeed in making a successful approach.

Background information about the customer and individual facts that may become available are valuable tools every step of the way. The amount and type of information, depends upon what you are selling and to what type of customer.

A sampling of the type of background information that could prove useful would include the following:

1. Raises in pay.
2. Promotions in position.
3. Outside interests.
4. Hobbies.
5. Sports.
6. Charitable Interests.
7. Community endeavors.
8. Fraternal organizations.
9. Facts about customer's industry.
10. Facts about customer's own firm.
11. Personal and family life changes.

Armed with this information, the professional salesman is in a position to call upon these facts to establish a proper footing for approach.

Previous unknown facts can be detected by the intelligent salesman with proper use of two of his primary senses, sight and hearing combined with intelligence. A visual, and not obvious check of the prospect's office and person can disclose much to the alert salesman. A sampling of indications of interests would include:

1. Plaques on the wall from organizations.
2. Pictures of hobbies such as boats, horses, etc.
3. Trophies, either loving cups or mounted on the wall.
4. Golf bag in room or tees on desk.
5. Lodge button or ring on person.

Both of the above groupings are samplings of the type of background information that could help.

Sources of background information include:

1. Who's Who.
2. Personal friends and neighbors.
3. Newspaper morgues.

16

4. Employees.
5. Co-workers.
6. Other salesmen.
7. Customers.
8. Competitors.
9. Office files on past history.
10. Employees of your hotel.
11. Local merchants or business men.
12. Business publications.
13. Various other fonts of information.

The amount of time spent in amassing this preliminary information should be in proportion to the item sold. A sale that could net $100 commission should not require or use three days of research. However, a certain amount of background can help to get any sale on the road.

Again, common sense is necessary to determine the sort of data that will prove most valuable in each case and with this arsenal of information on hand, you are ready to approach the customer.

Initial Impression

The initial impression frequently has a great deal to do not only with the success of the total sale, but with the basic question of whether you will have the opportunity to even proceed with your presentation.

Of primary importance is appearance. Most people like to deal with obviously successful people. The visible indications of success usually imply a greater ability or a better product. Hence, the pro gives off the aura of success "success breeds success." A professional salesman is smartly, but not gaudily dressed. His shoes are polished, his suit pressed, his shirt fresh, his nails clean, his face clean shaven, his hair combed, etc. This type of appearance tends to warm the prospect and instill confidence.

In keeping with personal appearance, the proper business card, engraved and not ostentatious will help create the right impression.

Most important, SMILE—do not grin but have a friendly smile.

Your first statement after introducing yourself should be aimed at gaining the attention and good will of the prospect.

This is the ideal time to make the previously mentioned visual survey of the customer's office and person. This survey will offer the clues to his interests and background for the next step in the approach. An intelligent inspection can confirm or correct previously conceived notions and supply new insights to the prospect. Does he have a mounted fish or moose head on the wall? Is there a loving cup with the statuette of a bowler or tennis player shown? All of these can answer questions for the next move.

Breaking The Tension

Frequently, at a first interview, a feeling of tension almost to the point of antagonism may emanate from the prospect to the salesman. The prime purpose of good appearance and demeanor is to eliminate any antagonism and reduce the initial tension.

The first statement after introductions are completed should be aimed at eliminating the balance of any tensions that may exist.

There is more than one *modus operandi* to accomplish this desired result. At this point we will discuss some of the methods that have proven most effective for the greatest number of salesmen and that should be mastered.

This is one of the first points at which the well prepared salesman can use his preliminary research. Once he has secured a knowledge of the prospect's special interests, he must get him to talk about them. Speaking of things close to one's heart, to an obviously interested listener, is extremely relaxing to most people and also will earn a great deal of good-will.

The usual method of starting this conversation is with a question. "I understand that you are a three handicap golfer. Have you ever played the Pebble Beach Course which is reputed to be so tough?" Or, "I heard that you were chairman of the Heart Fund Drive. Did you get the type of cooperation a cause like this deserved?" Or, viewing an evidence of a special interest in his office ask him about that.

Two words of caution. First, do not be too obvious in using this ploy. Secondly, do not be more than an interested listener unless you are extremely well versed on the topic yourself.

If none of the outside interest information is available, get a discussion started about his business. One's own business is always of interest. Do not do this with the trite "How's business?" but ask intelligent questions that are not impertinent but indicate a knowledge and basic interest in the field. A short anecdote (not disparaging) about another firm, in a different city, engaged in the same industry, is always interesting. General and new information about the industry in question can aid in achieving rapport. Be knowledgeable about the industry, its people and the latest developments. Even in imparting this information, at this point, try to start it in question form, such as "Have you heard about . . .?"

If you were able to establish any special motivations on the part of the prospect in your preliminary work, a remark aimed at these motivations may be the best maneuver.

Remember, to break the tension, the initial thinking and talking must be from the prospect's point of view and interests.

The telling of a funny story can also work very well, but one must be extremely cautious in the use of this method. Be careful in judging if this would be acceptable; be careful of any possible prejudice; be sure the atmosphere is proper for the telling of a story; never use blue or disparaging material; keep it short; and, most important of all, be good at telling stories. If you are not a seasoned raconteur, do not use this method.

Once the tension is broken, come back to the purpose of the visit as quickly as is possible. Do not stay on the subject too long. Remember, the only purpose for the approach is to get his attention for the presentation.

To determine which method of tension breaking to use, depends on a salesman's own preference combined with basic psychology. Properly judging the prospect's reactions, and complete flexibility in thought, are absolute necessities.

Leading Into The Presentation

As in all other facets of the sale, there is more than one usable method in leading into the presentation. Again, it will entail a combination of the use of one that suits the salesman best combined with judgment of the prospect's psychological reaction.

Arousing the customers curiosity with a specially planned question about one's product or service is usually good. For example, "Did you know that my product can do seven things no similar product can do?" Or, "Wouldn't a service that can reduce your payroll by 12% be of interest to you?" Plan the question carefully and be ready to demonstrate or make your presentation.

Another form of opening gambit that can lead into the presentation is the negative approach. This one should only be used by the real pro and under very limited conditions. This is preceded by a statement or question negating the customer's stature. Examples of this are: "I don't know if your company is big enough for this." Or, "Can your organization meet the qualifications we require?" Or, "I am not sure you have the ability or background to give us the cooperation we require."

When this method is used successfully, the prospect must sell you on his ability, finances, or stature before you will deign to make your presentation.

The simplest method and frequently the most effective is merely to tell him what you are going to do and then start doing it.

Gaining Undivided Attention

Very often a salesman will be confronted with the situation where a prospect is on the phone, reading a report, or correspondence, or working on books. When this situation arises, do not start your presentation until you have his undivided attention. Trying to reach the prospect and make your point over other disturbances will usually be a losing battle. Don't try it.

If the prospect continues to keep his interest on other items while you are in his office, redirect his attention.

Methods of accomplishing this end are quite simple. You can ask any question to divert his attention to yourself, and once you have it, start talking. Do not let him get back to his previous preoccupation. Another method is to suggest you wait until he is finished. If he says he can listen to you at the same time, be apologetic and say you do not want to distract him and would rather wait. A modicum of courtesy on his part will bring his head up and eyes on you. In extreme cases, ask for his attention outright. In no case should you be rude or should you offer to leave.

Retail Store Approach

As in the case of prospecting, the salesman in the retail store has no real problem with regard to the approach.

The basic impression factor is the same for all salesmen. He must be well groomed, smile, and emit a warm, friendly aura. However, planned methods of relieving the tension and leading into the presentation are not necessary.

A standard form of greeting and offer of help are quite adequate in this case. Greetings such as "Good afternoon," or "Good morning" will usually start the customer telling you what he is looking for. Other modes of approaching and addressing the customer are equally as mundane but equally effective. "May I help you?" Or, "Are you being taken care of?" will just about always get the desired result.

In the case of a browser thumbing through the merchandise, a slightly more sophisticated approach is advisable. Approach this prospect with pertinent information about the merchandise being examined either in the form of a question or a statement. For example, "Did you know that this merchandise has been marked down 20% for clearance?" Or, "These are the very latest imports, no other store in town has them yet." There is always some point of interest about the merchandise on hand.

All aspects of selling require the workable approach. Without a satisfactory approach, the number of opportunities to present your product and close will be greatly reduced. A pro salesman works out all possible approaches in advance and knows them as a second nature. If one does not seem to be working, he shifts gears and gets into another in a subtle and not too, obvious manner.

4

PRESENTATION

The preceding chapters dealt with prospecting and approach. These functions have only one basic purpose; to prepare for your presentation.

The presentation is probably the most important single facet of the sale and requires the greatest amount of preparation. A good presentation must set the stage for the close. It must tell or demonstrate to the prospect all of the important advantages of your product or service in relation to his needs. Citing advantages that have no relationship to the prospect's needs take unnecessary time, fills the air with extraneous information and detracts from the purpose of the presentation.

In addition to discussing the advantages of the product and its ability to fill all of the requirements of the specific prospect, the presentation must also create or expand the customer's need NOW. There is no close when a customer postpones action.

A great deal of preparation should be put into the preparing of a presentation. Part of this preparation, the product knowledge aspect, must only be done once. Other phases involve a continuing assembling of facts and information.

Good sales and marketing organizations recognize the importance of a strong presentation. Many thousands of dollars have been invested by sales minded companies to insure themselves that the presentation of their product will be much more than just adequate. On many occasions companies will not send a salesman out into the field until he has spent weeks or months in the plant learning all there is to know about what the company has to offer. Other organizations employ motion picture producers, technicians, actors, and writers to prepare a moving picture for the salesman to use in his presentation. Still other companies have slide presentations made to operate in conjunction with tape recorders or record players to get their presentations across in the most effective manner. Specially prepared samples are made for salesmen to enable them to demonstrate their products in their best light. Presentation books, artfully and psychologically planned, are again a tool to enable the salesman to motivate the prospect and prepare him for a close.

Obviously, large corporations do not make investments of this sort without expecting a return. They know that a good presentation is the key to the sale. The pro salesman knows this equally well.

The product knowledge factor of your sale frequently receives a good deal of help from the company. The onus of gathering the information for the other aspects of the presentation will, in most cases, fall on you. Do not short change yourself. Do the job.

Itemized below are the basic factors involved in the presentation. They include the preliminary information you gather, plus the features and icing you add to achieve the desired result:

Know Your Product

In the previous paragraphs that generalized about the presentation, we mentioned that the company frequently offered a tremendous amount of assistance to the salesman in amassing product knowledge. Use everything your company gives you and look for more.

Read and understand every piece of customer literature printed by your company, by any industry association, etc. Read and understand all salesman's literature. Subscribe to and read any and all trade publications regarding your product.

Other sources for additional product knowledge are:
1. Company buyers
2. Company engineers
3. Sales managers
4. Other and older salesmen (with clues to useage)
5. Catalogues
6. Competitors literature
7. All advertising matter
8. Reference books (in libraries)
9. Sales manuals
10. Outside schools (including correspondence schools)
11. Company training courses
12. Museums

Know your product as thoroughly as you can, not only what it is, but also what it can do. Be able to answer any reasonable question that might be put to you in as much detail as will prove necessary in each case. The correct and psychologically right answer can frequently lay the ground work to expedite the close. For example, if the customer asks the cost of operation, his mind is probably weighing your item against his present operation or against a competitor. If you have the right information about economies that can be effected, you may well have arrived at your close. A professional buyer may ask if an item is washable. If it is, the question may well have indicated that that was the prime requirement for a purchase. Questions covering ease of maintenance, potential uses, etc., may be put to you. Be prepared for them.

When you have an adequate amount of product knowledge, you are better able to give factual answers instead of generalities. This use of facts and statistics will engender confidence and can be the deciding factor in the sale.

If you were a potential customer for a mutual fund, how would you react to each of the following statements: "Our mutual fund is one of the best. We have been written up in many publications and have an outstanding record." This one was fairly good and the salesman who used it did well. The salesman who used this next one did better. "Our mutual fund has shown an increase in volume of at least 20% each year for the last ten years. We have been in the top ten for capital gains for each of those years. This outstanding record by our management has been written up in Barrons, The Wall Street Journal, and other financial publications."

Other examples of factual answers exist in all industries. Examples are "Our stamping machines are the fastest on the market." or "Our stamping machines can produce 7% more stampings per hour than any other machine of its type now made, and can produce equally as fine tolerances at this faster speed. In autos, details of mileage will produce greater results than just the words more mileage.

In answering questions about your product, show it in its best light, but be sure that you are truthful and control the tendency to exaggerate. If one factor is proven to be an exaggeration, the prospect will automatically assume that nothing you have said was reliable and you have lost the sale and probably lost the customer permanently.

Frequently, the product aspect of your presentation will serve as an education to the buyer. Do not overdo this function. Offer as much information as is necessary to show how the product or service fills his need or motivation but do not overwhelm him with facts that do not constitute an integral part of this particular sale.

In brief, know everything there is to know, use only that information that is necessary and pertinent to the specific sale and save the balance for back up and answers to questions.

Naturally, as in all other principals of salesmanship, different types of selling require greater or lesser degrees of product knowledge. A branded line of staples that are highly advertised such as cigarettes or detergents, being sold to the retailer, would not require the same degree of knowledge as the sale of computer services or sophisticated machinery to comptrollers or engineers and plant managers.

In the same vein the retail salesman's knowledge is frequently much less than it should be, and his sources of information from the firm also less plentiful. He can, however, make up for this shortcoming by using some of the sources enumerated earlier in this section. Other sources available to him are the buyer, labels on merchandise, instruction booklets with merchandise, and in some cases, the salesman who sold the merchandise to his store.

Additional advantages involved in having a sufficient amount of product knowledge will also accrue to the pro salesman and to the neophyte alike. Enough knowledge will enable the salesman to stress the important or best features of his product or service and put him in a better position to guide the prospect's thinking and attention. It will eliminate that element of fear in anticipating questions and objections and will thereby generate confidence. When you have the self assuredness of knowing all of the good points of your product you will exude this confidence and it must reflect in the buyer.

The product is the vehicle that satisfies the need, desire, or motivation of the prospect and converts the prospect into a customer.

Know Your Customer

Previous chapters, devoted to prospecting, and approach discuss in some detail getting to know the prospect. If this knowledge has been properly amassed, prior to the sale, it can be put to excellent use again in the presentation. Sources for gleaning this information were shown in the chapters referred to and repeating them at this point should not prove necessary.

The prime need for this knowledge is to determine the direction of the presentation.

Knowledge of a prospect's background and/or motivation will most often show a salesman the exact manner of presentation, or the type of product to be sold. An insurance salesman who knows that his customer is childless would not discuss a child's education policy but would, instead, concentrate on retirement or widow's benefits. If a buyer works for a bargain basement operation, a smart salesman would not try to push the most expensive and highest mark-up items in the line. Again, adequate knowledge of the prospect coupled with common sense will indicate the variations to be made in the presentation. Remember, and I repeat, a good presentation is the one that is aimed specifically at the prospect's need or motivation and kept within those guide lines.

If time allows, find out what makes your prospect tick. Learn which is his motivation button, and push it. Some of the more common motivations are listed here to give you a working knowledge of what to look for in aiming your presentation at the specific customer. Different ones, naturally, serve for different sales:

Most Frequently Encountered Motivations

1. Greed or profit
2. Status
3. Necessity
4. Security
5. Convenience
6. Pleasure
7. Fear
8. Altruism
9. Health
10. Personal complexes

One of these ten buttons will cause a reaction from just about anybody. Be sure to push the right one for each individual sale.

In addition to the preliminary work discussed in gaining the necessary information about the customer, close observance of customers reactions can prove to be an equally valuable tool. Your prospect's facial expressions, reactions or statements will outline any changes in your original plan of presentation.

Interspersing your presentation with questions can also give you clues to his reactions and the direction of his thinking.

To an observant and astute salesman, a customer's early reactions will show if he wants detailed demonstrations and explanations or just the highlights of useage with an explanation of how his needs will be filled. The salesman who talks too much for the specific prospect can frequently talk himself out of the sale. This is less prevalent when highly technical items are being sold to technically trained people. In other cases, however, the inner workings of an air conditioning system mean very little to the store owner. He only wants to know if it will work, cool his store, be touble free, and not cost too much.

The best way to organize the amount of information to impart is to imagine a scale in your mind. On one side put all of the facts you feel this particular prospect should and must have. From your store of facts, put the information onto the scale until it balances. In your personal warehouse you should have many additional facts. When he places a question, this question is placed on his side of the scale. You balance the scale by putting the answer on your side. Be sure to cover all salient points with reference to the customer, his needs, and motivations, but only add to this to maintain the balance.

Additional background that will help with the customer is a knowledge of his business. With adequate information here, you can talk from his point of view. This is usually very helpful in inducing the right frame of mind and attention. Use of trade jargon is not remiss here, but never use terminology or expressions that your prospect might not understand.

Once again, in discussing knowledge of customer, we come across the limited case of the retail store salesman. He has no opportunity to research his customer because, not being clairvoyant, he has no way to knowing who will walk into the store next. The retail salesman, as differentiated from the clerk, uses the tools that are available; primarily judgment, sparked with intuition.

These two tools are valuable and can work well, but, they are, too often, misused. Much too frequently, a retail salesman will prejudge his customer with no conversation and without making any attempt to sound him out. This can prove costly.

A personal experience of an associate of mine can best depict this. Walter—is an extremely successful building contractor with a seven figure net worth. His daughter announced her marital plans. For a surprise wedding present, Walter decided to build and furnish a home for the soon-to-be-married couple. Still wearing his mud stained clothes, that he wore to inspect his construction jobs, Walter walked into one of suburban New York's major department stores. Two salesmen in the furniture department studiously ignored him despite several attempts to get their attention. Had either of these salesmen shown the intelligence to speak to him, he would have learned that Walter wanted to purchase six rooms of the best quality furniture to be selected at the discretion of the store. Another salesman in another store, who overlooked the mud and got the prospect speaking, netted the biggest single order of his selling career.

The simplest first steps to aid the retail salesman to judge his customer is use the approach mentioned in a previous chapter. When the customer answers and tells what he is looking for, additional questions can help catalogue the customer. At this point the salesman can ask what he had in mind with specific questions relative to price range, type of merchandise, as advertised, etc.

When the answers to these questions are known, the pro retail salesman will know if the customer can be traded up or sold additional merchandise. The search for information, in this case, should not be a barrage of questions, but more in the form of suggestions interspersed with questions. For example, to a customer for a shirt. "In white, I have this broadcloth for five dollars, however, this Pima at $8.95 will always look better, feel more luxurious and last longer." "We have a special on these. By the box we sell them at three for $25." "How about a few of these new regimental striped ties to go with the shirts?" With questions and statements in this vein, the retail salesman can learn his customer's needs, appetites, and purchasing power.

In making your presentation, in all aspects of selling, the better you know your customer, the higher your ratio of success.

As in all other phases of the sale, the amount of effort and research invested in learning your customer should be in direct proportion to the type of sale and dollar volume involved.

Know Your Competitor

In itself, a full knowledge of your competition is not as necessary as the previous two aspects of knowledge. However, knowing your competition does frequently serve a valuable purpose in the presentation and is really an extension of your basic product knowledge.

Knowledge of your competition's product and price structure can give you confidence and eliminate the fear of questions. In fact, the salesman who has this knowledge and faith in his line welcomes the questions about the comparison of products because it gives him the opportunity to show his own wares in the most favorable light.

An important point with regard to the above paragraph is never insult your competitor or his product. There are several reasons for this bit of advice. Anyone who insults or abases another must demean himself in the eyes of his listener. You must be above this. Other reasons are that the prospect may be a personal friend of your competitor. If he is a sound business man, this friendship will not prevent his buying from you if your product is better. However, being badly critical of his friend may make him close his mind to your proposition.

Probably the most important reason for speaking well of your competitor is purely psychological. All people, whether they admit it or not, regard themselves as being intelligent. The possibility exists that the prospect may be buying or may have bought from your competitor. He knows he is too smart to buy garbage or buy over-priced merchandise or buy from people of questionable repute. Therefore, he may regard it as a personal insult if you imply that his other suppliers meet this description, because that would question his intelligence.

The best ways to handle questions about competition are the "They are good but we are better" method. Or you can damn them with faint praise.

Examples of these methods are: "They are a good company for a small one, but because of our size, production facilities, and purchasing power, we can supply more advertising, better prices, and much better delivery schedules." Or conversely, the small company representative can say "Oh yes, they are a good big company, but we are small and base our operation on personal service. We place a special value on each customer and your needs become our law." Again you can use the answer, "They make a good product that can do the job but look at the advantages in our product. These examples can continue ad infinitum, but I am sure the point is evident.

In the category of damning with faint praise, a different type of example can be used. "Yes, they aren't bad. I hear they have their production up to two units a week now." Or, "They are progressive. They even started to advertise now." I understand they have an advertising budget this year of $10,000—(when your company is known to have $1,000,000 or the like.)

No additional samples of these should be necessary. The use and application can be applied to any product or service. Use the "they are good but we are better" when you have better points that you want to point out. Use the faint praise when your better points are self evident and let the prospect feel that the knowledge of the advantages offered by your firm was a result of his own astuteness.

In knowledge of your competitor, you should not only learn the details of his product, management, production facilities, advertising, etc., but also his price structure for the same type of comparisons. Where price is a factor, this information does not require awaiting a question. An item can be shown or described with the quote "This is the only one at this price." Or, "This is the only one with these features at this price."

The use of comparative facts without being supercilious is also an accepted practice. "Our machine has these ten features, machine A only has six of them, machine B five of them, and machine C four," is an example of a clean use of comparison with competition.

With the suggestions shown here, knowledge of your competition is obviously an integral part of your presentation. However, stay within the limitations delineated. Do not assume a superiority that can cost you the sale.

The sources for information about your competitors are the same as most of the sources about your product. You can usually gain this information at the same time as you are amassing product information.

Most large companies, constantly publicize information about themselves. These companies frequently have public relations departments that are strictly involved with presenting the company image. In companies of this type, there usually are reams of printed information available. In smaller companies, the only sources of information are your employer, your co-workers, old customers, competitors, the neighboring community, and the trade and trade publications.

Sources for additional information about the large companies, in addition to the company's own literature, are reports and publications on corporations such as Standard and Poor's, Moody's, Poor's Registry, and Dun and Bradstreet. These sources are in addition to those that can be used for the small companies.

If your research turns up any detrimental or derogatory facts, get the details and get the answers that can put these facts in their most favorable light. It is better to be armed in advance, then to get hit with an unanswerable question that can destroy the presentation. Any unfavorable information always has extenuating circumstances. Good points or advantages that have ensued can outweigh the derogatory information. (We are assuming that you will be working for an ethical company.)

Basic facts that you should know are:

1. History
2. Growth
3. Principals
4. Stock information
5. Financial condition
6. Volume of sales
7. Manufacturing and/or service facilities
8. Advertising policies
9. Marketing programs

10. Customer relations
11. Forms of outlets
12. Personnel policies
13. Product lines (other than your product)

When you have this knowledge of your company, use it as the need arises in the presentation. Too much information along this line, to the prospect, can prove a bore unless he requests it. As a rule his prime interest is, are you financially sound enough to handle his business; have you indicated market acceptance by signs of growth; have you the facilities for his needs; are there are any factors that will help him such as co-operative advertising, etc. Do not volunteer any information beyond this unless requested, but if it is requested, be ready.

One final point on company knowledge. Some companies have established poor reputations for certain facets of their operation, poor delivery, inferior workmanship, etc. If this is pointed out to you by a prospect, tell him about the improvement, point out other good features. This is the one time when it is permissable to disagree with the prospect.

In the same token, it is incumbent on you, not only to disagree with unpleasant statements about your company from the prospect, but under no condition to make any disparaging remarks yourself.

This is one place where ingratiating yourself with your prospect will definitely cost you the sale.

Romance, Enhance, and Engender Enthusiasm

As previously mentioned, the purpose of the presentation is to show the prospect not only what your product or service can do, but how this is applicable to him and how it will fill a need for him. This can frequently be enhanced by using graphic means of presentation. Any factor that can create romance or enhance your presentation to make this point for the prospect is valuable. Any factor that can engender enthusiasm for your proposition should be considered.

Simple things can often work wonders.

An old saying in selling refers to a practice of some first class restaurants, "Sell the sizzle, not the steak." Many restaurants sell steak, but very few serve them on sizzling platters. Many companies make similar products to yours. Put a sizzle in the presentation of yours, create some romance.

Demonstrations are a prime method of building romance and enhancing a product in a customer's mind. The retail sporting goods salesman has the customer swing the golf club to create the atmosphere. The fur salesman tries to convince the female prospect to try on the fur coat. The beauty, luxury, and wonderful feel on her person may consumate a sale that all the words in the world could not accomplish.

In retail stores, the good sales person has samples of food or perfume for the customer. They suggest that the customer feel the fabric or run the sewing machine. All of these romance, enhance and create enthusiasm for the product.

In the case of sales other than retail merchandise, other tools are used and other guide lines followed.

Demonstration is still a great factor but do not over demonstrate. Frequently when a customer is given something to try on or see, he keeps his attention on the item and and salesman has lost control of the sale. To avoid this, point to the features you want to stress and retrieve the item. The romance is beautiful but it is a means, not an end. If necessary, use the excuse that you want to show him something else about the item to regain physical possession. If this method is used, have another feature ready to point out.

When selling an intangible, physical demonstrations are

obviously not feasible. There are, however, many other means of accomplishing the desired results of making dramatic demonstrations.

The use of graphic materials, all forms of printed literature, can be as effective as physical product demonstrations if properly used.

Different salesmen have different preferences in this mode of presentation. There are salesmen who prefer to use a presentation book or easel showing each point in order in the formal book. Other salesmen prefer to use individual sheets, making their points as they put each sheet on the desk. Either method is equally as effective. Caution should be exercised in the use of the second method to prevent the prospect from stopping the presentation in the middle by becoming engrossed in extraneous matter on one sheet. If this should happen, the best action on the part of the salesman, is to present the next sheet on top of the previous one being examined with an explanation.

Although the loose sheet presentation seems more informal, in actuality, each sheet is laid out in order and the presentation is exactly the same as that used with the formal book.

Other methods of romancing and enhancing the product are the use of comparative situations. The position of the prospect with the product and his comparative situation without it. If properly used, this can build enthusiasm for the product or service being offered.

If you romance your product or service properly, your prospect will begin to generate the same feeling. In the same manner, enthusiasms engenders enthusiasm. This was discovered many years ago by the snake oil salesmen and street corner pitch men. One of these small entrepreneurs could demonstrate or spiel his product for hours to a crowd that did not budge. A more enterprising member of the craft had the thought of hiring two or three shills who ran up enthusiastically to buy the product. The enthusiasm created by these shills was passed to the balance of the crowd who then also became purchasers.

This strong suggestion of enthusiasm does not require a shill for the pro salesman. His own enthusiasm in romancing his product can create all of the necessary enthusiasm on the part of the prospect. In short, no matter how many times he has told his story, no matter how many prospects he has seen, the good salesman never loses his enthusiasm and never stops generating it to his next prospect.

Additional knowledge of your proposition can help regenerate enthusiasm. Additional knowledge can give you more features over which you can wax enthusiastic.

Other tools made available by marketing minded companies help create and maintain the romance and enthusiam, and also enhance presentations. This includes the films and slides mentioned earlier. Group presentations and party plan sales are methods used for this end. The good salesman uses all of the good tools at his disposal.

Create A Yes Atmosphere

All aspects of this presentation should lead to a yes at close. The presentation should guide in creating a yes atmosphere. Questions can, and should be used, but these questions should always be worded in such a fashion that no intelligent person would respond with a no. For example, the question "Would you like to retire at the age of fifty five?" might evoke a yes or no answer. The door is left open for the negative response. To avoid this possibility, reword the question to force the yes. The question should have been put in this fashion, "If you decided that you wanted to retire at the age of fifty five, wouldn't it be a pretty good deal to be guaranteed an income of $550 per month for life?" The second question can only call for a yes. Do not permit the presentation to get the customer inured to saying no to you.

Help the prospect form the right habit patterns in his association with you. The best habit he can form is the habit of agreeing with you and saying yes to you. Establish and strengthen that habit for him.

There are several routes to establish this desired result. Any or all of them should be used. A series of questions should be planned to be interspersed in the presentation that will always call for the yes answer. Nod your head in assent while asking the question. In most cases, you will find the prospect will start nodding with you. The effect of this can be almost hypnotic.

One weakness evinced by many salesman in their presentation is the opening of the door for negative thoughts. Proper customer knowledge will aid in avoiding this potential disaster, as will proper wording. In referring to future benefits to the prospect, the word "When," should be used, not "If." The statement should say, "When you buy this," or "When you use this," not "If you buy this," or "If you use this."

Other negative thoughts are created by the thought of trouble. The only time the word trouble should be used in referring to your product is to say, "Trouble Free," or its equivalent. The statement, that your item will give less trouble than others, still plants the idea of trouble in the prospect's mind and trouble is negative.

The creation of a positive reaction in the customer's mind is actually based on the theory of hypnotism and should be used as such. The nodding of the head and the yes habit, as previously mentioned, are the first examples of its usage. The continued power of suggestion, iteration, and reiteration are tools of the hypnotist and are tools of the good salesman. Asking the prospect to perform minor inocuous acts, such as "Please hand me that paper" will start the habit of obeying your requests in his behavior patterns.

Be sure the prospect is with you all of the way. If the first presentation of your facts does not get the desired reaction, try to repeat it in different words. Mr. Hill, former head of American Tobacco Co., found these truths in repetition and in reiteration in the mass action created by his advertising programs. The salesman is not attempting anything as grandiose as mass hypnotism by the printed word. His only aim is to sway the prospect to his line of thinking and to close the sale.

Create A Sense Of Urgency

If the presentation is good and successful, it should not only create the need or desire to purchase, it must also create a sense of urgency, a sense of need now.

There are many propositions that cannot be sold at the first presentation and do require follow ups. However, the pro salesman knows you cannot enjoy spending money that you haven't earned as yet. The sale must be today to be a sale. Experience has shown that a promised order next week may well never be an order at all and no firms accept "maybe" orders on the salesman's report of activities as a *fait accompli.*

Other reasons for creating the sense of urgency are based on human nature and psychology. Once a person has signed an order or committed himself formally to a purchase, he has a feeling of obligation. However, if the obligation or final close are not established, buyer's remorse frequently sets in, and the sale is never consumated. Other chances of lost sale are the encorachments of competitors and the other uses that can arise for the available funds.

To avoid all of the above negatives, the sense of urgency must be established and maintained into the close.

Proper thought must be given to all of the factors mentioned here and full knowledge accumulated. The facts that make up the presentation information should be thoroughly known. With the knowledge in hand, the best presentation strategy can be planned. Under no condition should it be memorized by rote. A successful salesman must be flexible. The prospect's reactions and questions can indicate entirely new interests and motivations and the presentation could be much more effective in another direction. If the strategy is not memorized, the salesman should be fluid enough to change course when these other facts become evident.

In making your presentation, the use of questions has great value. The asking of questions enhances prospect's participation, relieves boredom on his part, indicates his point of view and motivations and gets him thinking along the lines you wish to establish.

If the prospect is the type that needs ego blostering, an excellent strategem is to ask his advice on several points. This will create some degree of self importance and a hidden feeling of gratitude to the salesman who helped establish his importance.

Some of the salient points to remember about the presentation are: keep away from controversial subjects; aim presentation at the prospect's needs, motivation and point of view; be lucid and make sure you are fully understood; speak well; use all necessary selling tools at your disposal; be sincere; do all of the necessary preliminary work and presentation work in proportion to the product or service sold.

5

HANDLING OBJECTIONS

Objections, and the methods of handling them, are in actuality a division of the presentation and should be studied in that context.

There are two prime reasons for not including this subject in the previous chapter. These reasons are based on the different times objections may be raised such as in approach, in presentation, or in close, and also the emphasis that should be placed on this facet of the sale.

In essence, adequate preparation of your presentation material should arm you with most of the necessary information necessary to handle objections. However, the techniques involved in using this knowledge are very important and must be learned.

A poor approach will almost always cost you the opportunity to make a productive presentation. An inadequate presentation is almost certain to cost you the opportunity to close. Mishandling objections can also be a factor in losing a sale. For this reason, it is necessary for the competent salesman to understand and be able to analyze the nature of objections and with this knowledge, handle any objections that may arise so that he can either effectively divert them, negate them, or use them as a tool to achieve a sale.

The first step in this process is to fully understand the nature of objections and the reason for their being raised.

According to the dictionary, an objection is a reason or argument against something.

In a sale, an objection, on the surface, is the reason or argument against hearing the presentation, against the product, or against making the purchase. This is superficial or surface appearance. In actuality, seeming objections can prove to be many different things and indicate different lines of reasoning. The skillful salesman will bring all of this out.

The emergence of an objection on the part of a prospect frequently demoralizes the neophyte salesman. Its affect on the pro is quite the opposite and, in fact, is often welcomed.

Early in my sales career, my mentor and employer was a man named George McLaughlin. George was instinctively a great salesman and a pro. Without ever having made a formal study of salesmanship, he had learned all of the necessary steps involved in consumating a sale and he used them. He did not attribute any nomenclature to these steps but he knew what they were and they were indelibly printed on his mind.

I had occasion to ask George about the handling of objections. It required several minutes for an explanation of the term objection. The answer is a quote I will always remember. "I often welcome objections. Usually a customer will object himself right into buying."

The thought George tried to express in that short sentence was that objections are often a tool in the hands of the salesman to enable him to lead to the close.

Objections arise before, during, and at the end of the presentation.

Nature Of Objections

An objection that is presented before the presentation is frequently a subterfuge to prevent or negate the presentation; to eliminate any mental obligation to buy; to indicate a fear of the salesman's salesmanship; to stall the salesman; to indicate antipathy to the salesman or his proposition; or to cover the prospect's defensive attitude.

The objections that arise during and after the presentation are less likely to be subterfuge. They may or may not be valid, but they are based on a fact, a questioned statement or an opinion. All must be handled effectively or the sale can be lost. Whether the expressed objection is valid or emotional or based on misinformation, it is still real and fact in the prospect's mind. Because of this, it must be treated with respect to avoid building up antagonism.

As a rule the salesman's fund of information about his product is much greater than that of the prospect. With this warehouse of knowledge, he can usually prove the prospect wrong or argue him out of his point of view. Either of these methods will correct or enhance the prospect's knowledge and will be sure to lose the sale for the salesman.

Never, under any circumstances argue with your prospect. Any argument, no matter how correct your position may be, must create antagonism and recriminations. Nobody can feel cooperatively disposed towards someone with whom he has just argued, especially if he lost the argument. Remember, you are there to sell the prospect, you are in a place of business, not trying out for a debating society. Another old but true sales platitude is "Win the argument, lose the sale."

In the same sense, never tell the prospect outright that he is wrong or infer that he is not too bright. These modes of handling objections may get the right information across but they are completely insulting and can destroy any rapport that might exist between the prospect and salesman.

A great deal of tact and subtlety must be used in handling objections. We will discuss some of the proven methods later in this chapter.

The first thing to remember about objections is that they are not always negatives. Frequently points that are raised, that seem to be objections on the surface, are points of an entirely different character or points with a different purpose.

Many times a so called objection is only a form of a request for additional information. Some people prefer to advance these questions as a negative to get the answer more succinctly. If this is the nature of a specific objection, it is to be welcomed because it will help emphasize a point that has the prospect's interest.

Often the objection is a disguised form of a request. It can be a request for a reason to buy. There are many timid prospects who really want to give you the order. However, they might require reassurance that they are doing the right thing, that buying your proposition is their best move. This objection is no more than a plea for you to convince them that they should sign the order.

Again, what appears to be objections, may be expressions of viewpoint, which can be easily and tactfully altered. Or they may be evidences of pre-conceived prejudices or opinions, and not be, in any way, associated with your present presentation. Eliminating this type of objection is only slightly more difficult but is necessary to assure attention and open-minded reception for your proposition.

Although objections may occasionally serve a purpose, and usually indicate that you have the prospect's interest and attention they are not to be sought and encouraged. To reiterate, even though objections afford the salesman the opportunity to correct misapprehensions and stress points of interest, it is best to avoid them. These advantages can be gained with normal questions from the prospect and leading questions to the prospect. Any negative aspect in a presentation should be avoided if possible. However, if despite the salesman, they should arise, they must be treated. They can be subtly negated, minimized, diverted, used to advantage, or answered in any other fashion. They cannot be ignored.

Methods Of Handling Objections

Under no conditions should the salesman evince trepidation or consternation with respect to objections. If these reactions become evident, the prospect assumes the negative thought was correct and no verbal answer can disabuse him. If a salesman is properly prepared with the necessary information discussed in the chapter on Presentation, including information about product, competition, company, etc. he should know the right answer and should be able to exude confidence.

Although the point is stressed not to encourage objections because they are negatives, the point was also stressed not to ignore them. In the same line of thought, do not delay too long in meeting them. When an objection becomes visible, take care of it as quickly as is practical in the presentation. Do not let an objection stew in the customer's mind. If he keeps the objection as a negative or derogatory thought for an appreciable period of time, it becomes ingrained and takes root. Under these conditions removal may become almost impossible or, in any event, becomes a major operation.

Each product or service normally has certain objections that keep arising. These objections become almost standard. The smart salesman learns these objections and anticipates them. For example, if you know that a large proportion of your prospects interrupt your presentation to complain about the shape of your product which may offer advantages because of its shape, advantages unrecognized by Mr. Prospect, do not wait for the objection before handling it. Incorporate the answer in your presentation. Anticipate and prevent the negative. A statement such as this will illustrate: "Notice the shape of our product. This was developed by our designers so that it can be used in such a fashion or accomplish specific tasks." Anticipation of this type can frequently become an added selling feature and will always help prevent negative thinking.

When any of the more prevalent valid objections encountered do not have a strong explanation, but really indicate a weak point in your presentation, then anticipation cannot be as effective. A good salesman does not stress negatives. In this case the best preparation is to have the best possible answer available to use when the objection arises. Examples of this would include answers such as, "Yes, it is quite small but that does not reduce the efficiency. We made it smaller to meet the price requirements." Or "You are correct, it is a lighter gauge metal, however engineering studies have proven that this gauge will give the same usage and will not be subject to any greater degree of depreciation." Whatever your explanation or answer, it must make sense, be sincere, and be readily available in your mind.

In the case of valid objections that can only be answered in the weak manner indicated in the previous paragraph, the full answer should also cover advantages. Add positives to give total weight. In this case the quote about gauge would continue "And even though the gauge is light, this machine can perform all of these additional functions which no other machine of its type can do."

The best answer to specific objections is a "Yes, but." In this fashion you avoid becoming argumentative and can still make your point. This can be done in many forms. An excellent way of making your point is to compliment the prospect on his analysis of the situation but these facts do not apply in your case. "That is an opinion many purchasing agents have had—But—." "That is usually true, but in our case" etc.

When the objection is completely valid and there is no gainsaying the prospect's point concede this point and immediately start enumerating all of the good factors that outweigh the subject of the objection.

Quite often a prospect will be wrong when he disagrees with a claim or a statement made by the salesman. Do not say "You do not know." Instead use the statement "You have been misinformed." This removes the onus from the prospect and the small nuance enables him to retain his self respect.

One of the most common objections encountered by salesmen in many fields is the objection to price or cost. When this objection is presented at approach, this constitutes the rare case when an answer must be postponed. Treatment such as, "I do not know if you have all of the facts about cost, and I will be pleased to discuss it after showing you the details of our proposition." Or, "We have alternate cost structures, when you see our proposition, you will see what I mean." At this point go into your presentation and answer the cost objection before the close.

There are several good methods of handling the cost or price objection when you get to them. One of the most effective is the pencil and paper approach. Run up figures and details to show that the proposition actually effects a savings or is cheaper in the long run.

Another form of handling cost or price objections, in fact a valuable method used to handle most types of objections, is the comparison method. There is an old saw that "Comparisons are odious." This is not true in handling objections. There are two completely different forms of comparisons that can be used. One is the comparison of your proposition with competition. The other form of comparison is the position of the prospect's company with your proposition—and his situation without it and making the advantages obvious.

Objections that are aimed at your product or company can be handled by comparison of the customer's present business with another organization that he may respect or admire. At this point testimonial letters are a great asset. It is an excellent bit of preparation for salesmen to have several letters of testimonial available to produce at an opportune moment. Testimonial letters in generalities and some that cover specific details can prove of great value in overcoming objections.

Logical progression of thought, even semi fallacious logic can also produce the desired result in this facet of the sale. That is if A is a fact and B is a fact, then obviously C must also be true.

On certain occasions, with a limited number of prospects, an objection can be used as the basis for a close. To wit: "Are those your only objections, Sir?" If the answer is "Yes," proceed in this fashion; "If I can show you the answers to all of these questions, to your satisfaction, then I assume you would buy this from me." In this case, all but very strong minded prospects will close their own sale.

Summary

To summarize, objections often are negative thinking, but this is not always the case. In no event do you handle an objection as the basis for an argument. Get the prospect's point of view, partially agree with him and then answer him.

Advantages are also realized when objections are raised. If the salesman knows the negatives that exist in the prospect's mind, he has the opportunity to correct them. If they are not expressed, they may be the cover that kills the sale. Objections give the salesman the clues to the thoughts of the prospect and help him aim his presentation. They also offer a salesman an opportunity to stress and repeat his stronger points.

In short, when you do encounter objections, make the most of them.

6

CLOSING

A great deal of time and effort is normally expended in prospecting. After the prospect is found and an appointment is made, the salesman must go through all of the other steps involved in the sale. A good approach must start him on the way to making an effective presentation. Objections must be tactfully handled, adequate interest and enthusiasm must be generated, and all of the do's and dont's in preparing for the sale must be closely observed.

With all of this effort and background work expended, nothing has been accomplished until the order is signed.

Every word, every paragraph, every chapter of this book served only one purpose. That purpose is the, "Moment of Truth." This is the time that the salesman asks for and receives the order. If the prospect does not become a customer, if the prospect does not buy, all of the preliminary work is lost.

In the cold hard facts of business, there is no pay off on sales that were not made. The properly prepared salesman closes the largest proportion of sales.

No salesman can close all of his presentations. However, a pro salesman is a closer and closes more sales than the run of the mill. Closing techniques combined with proper instinct are a decided factor in determining which salesman will be in the 20% group that does 80% of the business.

The instincts and technique can and should be developed.

The instinct that is referred to in sales circles as the tiger instinct is of prime importance. This is a necessary attitude and consists of never accepting the first "No." It is the instinct that keeps the salesman coming back again and again with new tactics, new openings, new thoughts, until he gets the "Yes" he is seeking.

Many prospects refuse to purchase upon the first request. Continued effort on the part of the salesman can often eliminate that refusal and change the prospect to a buyer.

As a matter of fact, the first "No" does not necessarily mean no. It can mean maybe, it can mean I think so, it can mean I am not fully convinced, or many other things instead of no. As long as the possibility exists that the no is not final, the salesman must never accept it and cease his efforts. No harm can befall the salesman for continuing to try. On the other hand, not getting an order that was available, is the worst economic and career harm that can occur. The top salesmen know they must close and they never lower their sights from that one goal.

Other traits that are necessary throughout the sale but meet their greatest demands in the close are persuasiveness and sincerity. If the "no" was reasonably final, good closing techniques combined with these traits can possibly reopen the door.

Certain types of sales are always closed on the first presentation if they are to be closed at all. Others may require additional meetings. This is especially true of high priced items or where the proposition will cause major changes to the prospect. In the sales that may require multiple presentations, the tiger instinct must be tempered to avoid creating a permanent antagonism.

If the prospect's motivations were fully known for the

presentation, etc. they should be used in the close.

Attempts at closing should not be limited to that point in time when the presentation has been completed in full. At any time in the sale that the salesman's intuition tells him the prospect is ready to buy, an attempt to close should be made. If these first attempts, and later ones fail, the salesman should go back to the presentation and try again at the next opportune time. At this point, those items that seemed to be of prime interest to the prospect should be stressed.

Closing can prove less difficult with full knowledge of techniques and of customer motivation. In addition, if the presentation also concentrated on the yes atmosphere and if the small habit patterns of obedience had been established as previously mentioned, this too can simplify closing.

Causes Of Negative Response

There are many causes of negative response and refusal of a prospect to close. Some of these are firmly based, others imaginary, others subterfuge based on a definite intention not to accept the proposition but without a logical cause. Listed below are some of the most prevalent reasons and the probable causes or lacks that bred these negatives.

1. Prospect cannot afford. Actual situation. (Indicates poor prospecting).
2. Prospect cannot afford. Imagined. (Indicates inadequate presentation or failing to handle an objection.)
3. Prospect unable to come to a decision. (Sense of urgency not created.)
4. Fear of making wrong decision. (Inadequate presentation or weak closing.)

5. Prospect dissatisfied with proposition. (Inadequate presentation.)
6. Cannot use product. Actual fact. (Indicates poor prospecting.)
7. Cannot use product. Imagined. (Inadequate presentation or failing to handle an objection.)
8. Prefers competitors product. (Inadequate presentation and lack of knowledge of competition.)
9. Temporarily committed in other direction. (Sense of urgency not created.)
10. Must submit proposition for approval. (If not a ploy, unavoidable.)
11. Do not want to commit themselves to a future action. Undecided about future trends. (Inadequate presentation and sense of urgency not created.)
12. Prospect not convinced of value of item. (Inadequate presentation and lack of motivation study.)
13. Requires initial action that is onerous to prospect. i.e. Spend too much; change resources; commit to specific responsibility; etc. (Did not appeal to motivation.)

Obviously, the causes indicated in the parenthesis in the above list are arbitrary. The onus does not always fall on the salesman or his lack. However, these causes are a result of poor salesmanship, often enough, to be mentioned, and a salesman should always be on his guard. Loss of sales because of the salesman's inadequacy should be corrected. There are occasions when the salesman's product is sub standard and the prospect knows it. That salesman should strive to get a line in which he can have faith and about which he can be enthusiastic. It is the poor workman who blames his tools.

Most Effective Closing Techniques

There are many techniques that can be used by a salesman to close a sale. Not all of these will fit all types of sales. Some also, are not applicable to every salesman's method of working or to his personal preference. However, most of them should be known by all salesmen. With this knowledge, the salesman can then select the most appropriate technique and achieve the best results.

Listed below are some of the most effective closing techniques and examples or descriptions of their use. You will notice that there is a similarity between several of these. However, a closer study will show that there are nuances that create a difference in their usage. In any event, for success, know them all:

1. Assumptive close—This is an automatic close. This close is based on the assumption that the prospect is in full accord. This simple close works very often. However, if the prospect balks, you can go on to one of the other closes with no harm done.

The assumptive close can be used in many fashions. An example of this close is to take out the contract or order form and pen and question him as you fill it out. Questions such as "Do you spell your name with an A or an E?" Or, "Shall I include your wife's name?" should be used. All during this time you should be busy writing, filling in the order or contract. If he does not stop you, he has committed himself to sign.

Another example of the assumptive close is to take out the contract, go over each point and detail, explain in full, and hand it to the prospect with a pen for signature.

An additional version of the assumptive close is the alternative commitment close. This is very similar to the assumptive close but is based on giving the prospect an alternative in his purchase.

Examples of this can be shown with questions such as, "Do you prefer the large size or the smaller?" "Which of these services will fill your needs better?" In this close, when the prospect selects an alternative, he commits himself.

2. Oversell and undersell close—This is another form of close that quickly induces the prospect to commit himself to buy.

This close is based on an apparent attempt to oversell and causes the customer to correct the salesman and state his needs, thereby giving the order.

A simple case in point is the salesman who, knowing the customer can use one dozen of his product, will say "You should purchase five dozen as an initial order." The prospect will naturally object and say "I cannot use more than one dozen." At this opportunity the salesman can reluctantly agree and state, "All right, we will put you down for one dozen." The customer feels he scored a victory, but he did buy.

3. Ask for the order close—This is as easy as it sounds and frequently works well. If the presentation was well accepted and motivation met, close with the request for the order. A simple statement such as "If you will give me your check now, I will start service or ship on   date."

A note of caution. This close must be handled in a very open manner. You have a good product or service at a good price and the prospect can use it. Never lower your dignity. Never plead for the order or attempt to ask for an order by trying to evoke sympathy.

4. Objection close—This was explained in the chapter on objections. If a prospect has one major objection, the salesman asks, "Is that your only objection?" If the answer is in the affirmative, the salesman comes back with, "If I can show you that this is an objection without foundation, then I see you will buy my proposition." The customer is fully committed at this point if the salesman has a satisfactory answer to the objection.

5. Negative close—This works on the same principal as the negative approach. This is used where ex-

clusivity of area are given or specific performance is required from the prospect.

The salesman using a negative close words his statements in this fashion; "I would like to give you this distributorship but I am not sure you can fulfill the quota." Or, "Do you have the sales staff necessary or the production facilities to perform these actions?" Or, "This is a wonderful machine we offer, but it is only for big operators, I am not sure you are big enough to use it."

If the salesman's judgement of the proposition and the prospect were correct, the prospect will then find himself selling the salesman to permit him to be a customer.

6. Reiteration with self closer—This is only useable when a prospect asks many pertinent questions and receives the answer that completely answered his reservations and motivations. At the end of the presentation, the salesman reiterates all of the points covered in the questioning and indicates that there is absolutely no reason to delay signing the order.

In using this close the salesman repeats all of the salient points raised and closes in this manner: "We fill this specific need that you expressed, we also fill these needs as I've shown. Our delivery is within your schedule, etc. There is the order form."

7. Psychological obligation close—This is a close that the author has never used, but for which others may find advantageous situations.

This close is worked in two steps. A point is made in the approach or early in the presentation to put the prospect into a position of psychological obligation to the salesman and is repeated at the close. Samples of this are; "I was going to start my vacation today but I knew how badly you needed my product, so I postponed the holiday." Or, "Knowing your position in the industry, I travelled six hundred miles just to show you how we could help you." etc.

8. Status close—This is a close that caters to the prospect's ego and is applicable in the sale of prestige products or services. The basis is in the statement, "How can a man in your position not purchase this?" Or "How can a company such as yours, that is such an important factor in the market, pass up this proposition that would enhance your position so much more?"

This is also a keeping-up-with-the-Jonses close.

9. Favorable comparison close—This is a first cousin of the status close. Statements that best depict this close are: "This is the model that firms such as   and   have bought." Or, "All of the more intelligent buyers have selected that one." Or, "I have found that those firms that are most successful usually start with three units. I'll put your order in for the same."

10. Unfavorable comparison close—This close is based on the unhappy history of others. In the poor comparison close, the salesman points out sorrowful stories of people who delayed and the loss or additional cost that resulted. This close is most effective in insurance and sales that entails improving or upgrading the prospect's present situation. The type of statement used in this close is, 'Every day you delay you leave yourself open to be passed by competition, such as happened to   in   city. Or "As you know, Jones Co. were the leaders in their market until Smith Co. took in automatic production equipment. Now Jones has lost their position and are also-rans to Smith. I strongly urge you not to delay. Be a Smith type of company, be a leader. Do not lose out like Jones did."

Naturally salesmen selling items such as sprinkler systems, insurance, and improved production facilities are the ones that will use this close most frequently.

11. Last chance close—Sometimes called limited opportunity close. This close must be used very subtly and very tactfully or it can be an insult to the prospect's intelligence. Although the close is usually based on an honest fact, there are salesmen who use it in a bluff.

In addition to subtlety, customer psychology enters into play in this close and prospect's reactions must be judged accurately. The close is based on a changing situation and would be covered in statements such as "This is the last opportunity to buy at this price. Next month this item will be 10% higher in cost." Or "These are the only two we have in stock, we do not know if we will be able to import any more." Or, "Let me protect your position by putting your order in now, after these are sold we will discontinue the line because production is too expensive."

12. Loss of advantages close—This is a close that is aimed at eliminating a delay. The basis of this close is that the prospect will buy sooner or later, but while hesitating or waiting, he will miss all of the advantages available in the interim.

Samples of this close are best exemplified by these statements; "During the period that you are waiting, you will lose out on the additional production or protection it will afford you. You know that you will need it at a later date in any event, why not take it now and enjoy these advantages in the interim?" Or "All of the other manufacturers will get the jump on you in this new method of production while you are waiting. Do not lose the advantage you now hold. Purchase and use this new machine now and you will have it available when you change over your production line."

13. Economic close—This is actually two different closes but both based on dollars and cents.

The first is the obvious fact that the proposition is actually inexpensive for the savings or advantages that are offered.

The other is similar to the Loss of Advantages Close. In this case, the salesman uses a pencil and paper to show all of the financial advantages that would accrue to the prospect if he bought now and also the continued dollars and cents advantages for the future.

14. Logical close—This is a step by step progression in logic. It is similar to the use of logic mentioned in the handling of objections and must be thoroughly thought out. It is based on a series of statements or questions such as; "You will admit that A is a fact, won't you?" Next, "As you can see, B is also a fact, isn't it?" And a final statement is the close "Well, if A and B are facts then C is obviously true and it would make sense for you to buy my proposition to satisfy this great need." A similar way of showing these quotes in an actual case would be; "You tell me that the cost of this proposition is no great barrier in your case, is that not so?" Next, "As we have agreed, you have a strong use for this proposition and purchasing it can enhance your position, isn't that correct?" In that case why delay, you need it now and there are no reasons not to consumate the deal now."

15. The special offer close—This is a reverse of the Last Chance Close. It is only useable in conjunction with a special offer being made by your company. The basis is; "If you sign now, we will give you" or "We will reduce." etc.

16. Trial offer close—This is a close that is quite simplified but has ruined many potentially good salesmen. This close should only be used as a last resort but lazy or weak salesman use it as the

line of least resistance. The trial is based on a company policy that permits shipments on consignment or free trial offer or acceptance of small sample orders.

The correct useage of this close is based on an obvious no regular close being possible. As a last resort, the salesman suggests a small inexpensive sampling order or the free trial consignment.

The prime problem with the use of this close, in addition to tempting salesmen to be lazy, is the prospect's lack of financial involvement. Without this involvement, the customer may not give your item the full attention or display or effect it deserves and often has a negative result.

If no close is affected upon the first presentation, but a future close looks possible, try to pin the prospect to a firm appointment. Try not to leave with an "I will call," or "See you in about a month." If he permits the specific date, he again, partially obligates himself.

When the prospect must consult with another to reach a decision, make every effort to invite yourself to this meeting with the other party. Your prospect is limited by his memory and general knowledge of your product or service. He could not possibly depict it to a third party in as favorable a light as you can.

Again, if there is no apparent reason for refusal to buy, and no decision can be made as to what additional closes to attempt, use the simplest expedient. Ask the customer.

When the sale is closed the salesman should leave as soon as courtesy permits. It is an excellent idea to congratulate the customer on his decision but do not rehash the sale. Do not stay around and assume the risk of undoing any of the good work.

If no close has been effected, whether or not a future appointment has been arranged, thank the customer for his courtesy. Always leave with an open door.

7

SALES PERSONALITY

The most direct route to determine the answers to the supposed mysteries or intricacies of a sales personality is to first determine what constitutes the sales personality.

The dictionary defines personality as the personal or individual quality that makes one person be different or act different from another. Synonyms are shown as character or individuality. Common usage has added several additional ramifications. The word has come to cover personal habits, thinking, speech, vocabulary, voice, and any and all other traits that will have an effect on others. Also, as a result of general useage, unless negative adjectives such as bad personality, poor personality, negative personality, etc. are used, all references to anyone's personality indicate a good or favorable connotation. The phrase "He has personality" is complimentary.

Taking the above definition and applying it to the specific field of sales would still offer the same basic meaning except limited to useage in approach, presentation, answering objections and in closing.

In short, a sales personality would be the personal traits, the components of character and training that enable a salesman to project well; that enable a salesman to insure attention and cooperation; that enable a salesman to secure favorable reactions and actions from others.

The Myth About Sales Personality

For years most people were under a misapprehension of what comprised a sales personality. In fact, to this day, many people still have delusions.

The salesmen heroes of this myth were the complete extroverts, extroverted to a fault. When one thought of a salesmen, one conjured up a picture of garish clothes, boisterous voice, cigar in face, and the purveyor of the latest bar-room stories.

Even today, in a more enlightened period, the average person who is not in sales has created a new myth. Today's picture of a successful salesman usually evokes an extrovert. Although it no longer depicts garish clothes, he is still over dressed. The uninformed usually expects him to be a braggart and still have the latest off color jokes at his finger tips.

Part of this misconception is the illusion that all salesman are born with these mysterious traits of character and unless so endowed, one can not hope to be successful in this field.

All of these mistaken ideas are carried by a vast majority of people who are not in the sales field, or by others who have made unsuccessful forays into the art.

It is true that some people have as a part of their nature better and more outgoing personalities, more affable characteristics, more likeable ways and all of the components of a better personality which they apply to sales. However, good sales personalities do not appear only in those who were born or grew up with these traits. Others can develop them.

In short, a good sales personality is not necessarily a gift given to a limited few such as beauty or artistic talent. In very many cases, this desireable personality is an adapted improvement and the result of hard work and self discipline.

Components Of A Sales Personality

The components of a sales personality begin with what is obvious in the first visual reaction on the part of others. This is part of one's personal habits. If a salesman is always well groomed, clean shaven and tonsored, if his clothing is clean and well pressed, if his shoes are shined, then he has passed the first test. Visually he exudes a pleasant and satisfactory appearance and thus, personality. Even in this first step, there is a great deal of room for one's individuality to show. Many salesmen prefer their nails manicured, others just filed and cleaned. Some have full hair cuts, others crew cuts. Personal tastes in clothes can also be catered to as long as the finished product is business like.

After the first reaction, other components that make up the sales personality become apparent. Is the smile warm and friendly or is it a smirk or grin. A smile must not be a smile of the lips only, but must show in the eyes.

At this point, the first vocal evidence is shown. The voice should be well modulated and all evidences of illiteracy in diction and pronunciation avoided. A good vocabulary is also an important facet of the sales personality.

The saying of the correct things and avoidance of appearing to be self centered are important. Traits of personality that always leave an excellent reaction on others are showing proper respect without fawning, and showing a definite interest in others.

Sincerity is a desirable trait in the make-up of the sales personality. This combined with confidence, persuasiveness, determination, character, and dynamism make up the pro salesman who earns respect and higher income.

With varying degrees of effort, all of these can be achieved if they are not already a part of the make-up.

Developing A Sales Personality

Habit patterns are difficult to break. However, it can be done. The basis steps involved in developing a sales personality are the breaking of bad habits and the replacing of them with good ones. This takes self control, self determination, and will power. We all have enough of these traits. It is well worth our while to cultivate them. The goals are high. A person cannot automatically change, but slow improvement in outer evidences of one's character can result in establishing good habits.

To begin, an honest self inventory is necessary. Combine this with an inventory of successful salesmen that are worth emulating.

Are your personal habits in cleanliness and grooming desireable ones? If not, this is simple to remedy. Always be well dressed and well groomed.

The next personal observation may be more painful to the ego. Do you have any distracting or unpleasant habits or mannerisms? These can be most subtle and not necessarily only the more obvious ones such as nail biting and teeth gnashing. Many people are normally unaware of having these habits and it requires a close personal scrutiny to unearth mannerisms that drive others to distraction.

If an honest self inventory indicates the existance of these undesireable practices, break yourself of them at all costs.

Learn to develop an interest in others. If you can establish true empathy with those with whom you come in contact, you have taken a big stride towards sales personality.

Practice your smile. Literally spend a period of time every day in front of the mirror smiling at yourself. Do not discontinue this until you can honestly say to yourself that your smile is sincere, friendly and warming.

Your handshake should be firm but not a bone crusher. This too can be achieved with practice.

Your voice and speech habits can be cultivated and improved if you try. Speak in an empty room and use a tape recorder. Satisfy yourself that your voice and diction reach the desired levels. If your vocabulary is limited, practice can improve this too. Everytime you hear or read a new word, make a note of it and remember the context of its use. At the end of each day, look the words up in the dictionary plus additional new words selected at random from the dictionary to total a minimum of 20 new words a day. Write the words and their meaning down five times and repeat them aloud five times that evening. The amount of new words that will enter your vocabulary will astound you. Improving your reading habits will also be a helpful factor in conjunction with this practice.

Build your memory, if necessary take a memory course, but try never to forget a name or a face. This remembering is an endearing quality in the sales personality and failure to remember a name can, at times, cost a sale.

The balance of traits that must be developed to achieve an outstanding sales personality are traits of character. These must be worked at much more assiduously. You must be determined and concentrate on being whom you want to be.

Have faith in yourself and in what you have to sell. This will eliminate timidity and enable you to emanate an aura of confidence, enthusiasm and assuredness. This will enable you to also be truly convincing, sincere and persuasive. With these traits you can develop the strength of character to keep from yielding when you shouldn't and the good judgment to know when you should.

When your personality has the strength and confidence required, avoid the swinging of the pendulum too far in the opposite direction. Many people, who in this manner succeed in conditioning their thinking do develop all of these desirable traits. However some go to an extreme and find themselves with a new group of undesireable characteristics. They may become brash, opinionated, conceited, or exude a superiority complex. Keep taking inventory of yourself and see to it that you are who and what you want to be.

In very few words strive to have that indefinable asset called "class" and combine this with all of the other favorable characteristics that will enable you to motivate people.

To reiterate, all of this takes work and practice. A violin virtuoso achieves his high degree of success by long hours of playing and correcting. He starts with a hidden talent and brings it to its artistic heights by dint of hard work. Everyone has the talent of an obvious or latent sales personality. For those who want to achieve success in the sales field, this talent can be brought out or improved by the same type of effort.

8

FRANCHISE SALES

No book on sales would be complete in today's markets without some summary of franchising and franchise sales.

Definition of Franchise

As used in the commercial sense, a franchise is a license to operate under the name and style of the franchisor. In cooperation with other franchisees and having the opportunity to receive the training, guidance, benefits, national recognition, and savings that accrue to the franchise holder, the franchise offers the shortest route to a new business.

The franchise is paid for in many different manners. The most common of these being the franchise fee and/or royalties. However, other modes of reimbursement are used such as all purchases must be made from the franchisor or minimum inventory purchases.

Background of Franchising

Prior to World War II, the only franchises with which the average man was familiar, were automotive sales and drug stores. Since the end of the war, the franchise trend has been on a continuous rise with the greatest indications of growth being shown in the last five to ten years. Every type of business and service is now being franchised. From auto repairs to hospital rentals, from home cleaning to motels. Included in these franchises are such other industries as distributorships of chemicals and electronic products, car washes, cleaning stores, printing, painting, hearing aids, burglar alarms, closed circuit T.V., teenage night clubs, all forms of food sales including wholesale distributorships, drive-in restaurants and fine food establishments. Who, ten years ago would expect to see employment agencies, travel agencies, or fund raising franchised?

Articles and stories on the growth of the franchising field have appeared in the Wall Street Journal, Reader's Digest, McCalls, Elks Magazine, Changing Times, Mechanics Illustrated, Science and Mechanics, Prentice Hall News Letters, plus all the publications that have come into existence that deal only with the franchising field.

Advantages of Franchise

A good franchise operation offers many benefits to both the franchisor and the franchisee.

The advantages accruing to the parent company include:
1. Enlarge markets for products.
2. Introduction to new and future markets.
3. Elimination of personnel problems (as compared with self operated outlets).
4. Development of new and enhanced sources of income.
5. Sounding boards for new products.
6. Direct income from franchise fees and royalties.
7. Opportunity to expand nationally with limited capital outlay.
8. Savings effected by mass cooperative advertising and buying.

Some of the advantages to the franchisee are an opportunity to go into a business that he does not know, with a big brother image to teach, guide, lead, and help every step of the way. (This eliminates the fear deterrent and enables many more people to realize the great American dream of their own business). Another advantage is the opportunity to have instant recognition from the national image of the parent company. Also of importance are the opportunities to participate in cooperative or mass advertising, purchasing, etc. without the large capital outlay that is normally incurred in these programs. Additional savings usually result because of standardization and elimination of trial and error.

Prospecting in Franchise Sales

Prospecting in franchise sales has generally been more limited than in most other forms of creative selling. Majority of the new franchises being offered today are offered by advertisements in various media. From a national aspect, The Wall Street Journal and the Sunday New York Times plus periodicals devoted to franchising or specific industries seem to have the lead. However, local advertising for various franchise offers can be found in many local newspapers throughout the country.

The other prime method is intra-industry contacts. This is either writing, phoning, or visiting people in allied industries who might be interested in expanding their operations. For example, if you had a franchise to offer in a new floor covering or finishing, natural prospects to contact would be floor covering people, home improvement people, painters, lumber yards, etc. In a like manner, motel franchisors would contact real estate people, construction people, investors, and the like.

The first move in prospecting for franchising in this fashion, as in all other salesmanship, is a thorough analysis of the market and utilization of imagination.

Here again, the difference between the 20% on top and the 80% run of the mill salesmen will show itself. If the real pro failed to close a lead in a town, before moving on, he would determine what type of people in town could be likely prospects, check the yellow pages or other available directories, and see if he couldn't make the trip profitable and productive.

Methods of Sale

The methods of selling franchises vary considerably. Some of the most usual methods used will be outlined below.

1. The pilot operation: This is limited to a franchise that has really successful franchisees or self operated locations. Before final contact and closing is attempted, the lead is invited to go to some of these locations, see the operation, and examine the books. If a final appointment is made after this examination, a great deal of pre selling has been accomplished and closing proves much easier.

2. Pre qualified write ins: When many answers to an ad are received, covering a wide geographic area, the best method to save time and expense, is to pre qualify these leads. Send them literature that will whet the appetite and motivate action. Follow up the literature with a phone call or a series of phone calls to determine if the prospect is competent to handle the franchise. Then determine the degree of interest. If interest is strong enough, a personal meeting either in the prospect's town, or at the home office are almost always necessary to close.

3. Saturation advertising: This usually is within an affiliated industry as previously explained, but can be in local newspapers to the general public. In this case, a mail order campaign is usually necessary to the principals of all of the companies in affiliated industries. For example, a diaper service franchise

would contact all of the commercial laundries, hand laundries, coin operated laundries, cleaning establishments, companies selling baby furniture, baby photos, etc. However, a newspaper ad with return coupon would work for a less limited franchise. Initial contacts would give limited information and a reply card requesting information would be enclosed. Those that evince interest would receive additional literature and be further qualified on the phone. The franchise salesmen would then make a series of appointments, make a trip to the town, and attempt to close one of the prospects.

4. Hotel phoning: This may also be coupled with a phone in ad in a local newspaper. This method operates quite similarly to the above. In this case, however, the salesman travels to a town with no appointments in hand. Searching out the same type of prospects mentioned in paragraph number 3, he calls, gives a short phone presentation, and attempts to make an appointment. Phone-ins from the newspaper ads can be handled in the same fashion. These appointments can prove quite fruitful. Note: In methods 3 and 4, it is usually advisable for the salesman to have a prestige suite and to make his presentation in his hotel. The advantages are both psychological and tangible. First, there is added psychological strength in his own quarters without the connotation of a hat in hand solicitation. He is more firmly in the driver's seat. Secondly, there will not be any interruptions by employees, telephone calls, or any other problems that arise in normal business operations.

There are, naturally, many other methods of salesmanship and other techniques possible in franchise selling, however, those listed above are the most used and, to this point, have proven most successful and effective.

In this chapter, no mention is made of techniques of the franchise package, such as an A and B package or part payment package, etc. Although these are often important additional sales tools, they are tools that must be supplied by management and do not rightfully belong in this book.

Closing Franchise Sales

In the closing of a franchise sale, the same closing techniques discussed in an earlier chapter are applicable. However, certain techniques are more effective in franchising than in most other forms of sale. The negative close would obviously be most workable here. Close observation of your customer's reactions and questions should still be your guide.

One point to take into account in franchise selling is that without a great deal of pre qualifying, a franchise sale is very rarely a one meeting close. Even if the prospect is fully sold, the purchase of a francise is a major change in his way of life and it could well require discussions with his attorney, accountant, banker, family, etc. and frequently a credit check of your company will be necessary.

From the point of view of the salesman, franchise selling is truly creative selling and is high up on the income scale for the professional salesman.

9

ITINERARIES

Organizing Your Itinerary

Itineraries will vary greatly depending on the product or service being sold, type of market being covered, etc. For example, the retail salesman working in a department or specialty store will have no problems in pre-planning his day or week. The salesman who has many accounts in each town will, on the other hand, have to do a great deal of organization of time and travel, and the salesman who has a large territory with an exclusive one account in a town type of market will have a completely different set of problems.

As long as travel is necessary in your work, whether it be within the confines of one city, or across the country, there are certain basic rules that will help insure the greatest utilization of time and thereby the best results.

First and foremost, organize and plan your moves thoroughly. Secondly, plan a full series of alternates. These can be extremely important. For example, if you are working within the confines of one city and plan to work a special geographic location, take into account any parking problems you might encounter, distance between prospects, availability of prospects at the time you will be in the vicinity, etc., etc.

If a prospect is not available to you, have an alternate destination or stop available as nearby as is reasonable. In short, map out your day or week in full detail, but be fluid and set up alternate programs because you cannot always control the availability of your customer. Whenever possible, use the phone, mail, or any other means to set up advance appointments. This is one of the greatest time savers there is. However, this procedure is not always practicable.

For the salesman who travels on a wider scale, the same basic principals apply. Organize your trip, make advance appointments whenever practical, but have alternates available.

Here is an example of how use of alternates can save a full day's productive effort for the traveling salesman. A salesman selling just one account in a town reaches the St. Louis airport at 2:00 P.M. with the intention of going to Joplin, Mo. and then to Springfield, Mo. A check of available flights shows that Ozark Air Lines has a 2:20 P.M. flight to Joplin that arrives at 4:18 P.M. Obviously, a 4:18 P.M. arrival time, after waiting for baggage and riding into town, would entail an after 5:00 P.M. arrival time and would probably preclude conducting any more business during that day. A further check of the airline schedule shows that Ozark has a 2:20 P.M. flight to Springfield, Mo. that arrives at 3:43. That difference of 35 minutes could possibly be the difference between getting in that one more call in the day. With flexibility in planning, the wise salesman can switch his itinerary. In this case it was just alternating the order of travel to Springfield and then Joplin. A further check of the airline schedule shows a 6:42 P.M. and a 6:00 A.M. plane leaving Springfield for Joplin. This enables the aggressive salesman to get in one extra town and save a full day.

Examples of this type are as numerous as are air line schedules, but with solid planning and intelligent flexibility, a good salesman will get the most presentations out of his time and the axiom most frequently propounded by the Fuller Brush Co. is that the man who makes the most calls, makes the most sales. All other things being equal, this is obviously true. Hence, the wise salesman gives himself every reasonable edge.

The planning of the itinerary must take many things into account, not just the proximity of customers but also the weight of potential volume, as well as availability of accommodations, parking, transportation and all other details unique to each product or service. If there are five accounts who are each potential one thousand dollar customers in a cluster, and one potential ten thousand dollar user in a more isolated location, this may engender a different type of planning. Another feature to be considered in this case in rationing the salesman's time is the probability of closing in proportion to the time expended. Ultimately the answer must be where and how can my time best be used to bring the greatest results.

Determining Means of Transportation

Working within the confines of a city, the existing situation in public transportation, parking, proximity and locale of customers and all other features peculiar to the city will determine if auto, taxi, or mass public transportation are most feasible. This decision can also be affected by the size and weight of samples or collateral material.

In the realm of travel a proper analysis of the area to be covered and the degree of coverage will also produce the intelligent answer. A salesman working cities forty to fifty miles apart would probably be better off travelling by auto, especially if there were several stops to be made in each town. By the same rule of thumb, the salesman making stops hundreds of miles apart would probably be better off travelling by air and renting cars in the towns, if needed. These decisions, of course, might be altered when the cost of transportation is calculated in proportion to potential.

Again, nothing can be hard and fast. Alternates may be advisable. For example, flights between smaller towns may entail several changes or long waits, and a check of the local Greyhound or Trailways might indicate that a bus could get you to your destination hours earlier, or a rented car could be your answer. The big three of Avis, Hertz, and National frequently have cars available that you can rent here and drop off there with no drop off charge. The only costs to you would be the daily and mileage charges.

Making Air Line Reservations

Plotting your trip on a road map is reasonably easy. Planning your next move by air is no more difficult.

All of the air lines are extremely accomodating and as a rule, they will supply any one calling with all of the information he needs. If you were to call any air line, tell the reservations clerk of your point of departure and point of destination, and approximate time of departure, he will plan your flight for you. In most cases he will supply this service and make your reservations on other air lines if his air line does not have flights to your destination.

However, in planning an air itinerary and alternates, a complete set of scheduled information can often be of great help. A publication called the Official Air Line Guide is available for perusal at every air line counter or can be subscribed to by writing to Official Airline Guide, P.O. Box 6710, Chicago, Ill. 60680. This publication, issued twice a month to keep up with changes in schedules, lists alphabetically all cities reached by scheduled air lines. Beneath the names of the cities, an alphabetic list of cities of origin of all flights and the flight numbers, air lines, times of departure, times of arrival, type of equipment, number of stops and any other pertinent information. Using this guide makes planning the most practical itinerary comparatively simple.

An additional tip to the neophyte air traveler—it is always advisable to have reservations. However, if none are available, this does not preclude your getting on the plane. This author has come to the airport early and received a low stand-by number upon many occasions and in over 90% of the cases has traveled on a flight that had no reservations available.

Selecting and Reserving Hotel and Motel Accommodations

The selection of a hotel or motel should not be a haphazard, hit or miss selection. In this phase of your itinerary the selection can effect cost, success, and time. Questions that must be answered cover many phases of your activity. For example, will the customers have occasion to meet you at the hotel? In that case a prestige hostlery with ample parking is necessary. Do you have your own transportation? If not, a downtown location is best, and also a restaurant and lounge on the premises are advisable. If you have transportation, a location nearest the concentration of customers might be best. Do you make your presentation in the hotel? Most accommodations catering to commercial trade, to any degree, have meeting rooms, sample rooms, studio rooms, etc. Before determining your hotel, take all of these factors plus accessibility, room price, and all other requirements into account.

Full information on the better rated hotels and motor inns can be found listed geographically with ratings in the A.A.A. Travel Guides, Mobil Travel Guides, and

Shell Travel Guides. There are probably other sources equally as qualified available but, the above are more than adequate. These publications describe the accommodations, facilities, etc.   •

As a rule of thumb look for air conditioning and telephones in all rooms. Parking, a description specifying modern rooms and furnishings, swimming pools, restaurant on premises, meeting rooms, are also indications of first class accommodations. Geographic location with regard to downtown, air port, and major highways will also help you make your decision. A combination of these factors and the rating given by the travel guide are your best information.

As you travel, you will become familiar with the various chain operations in the hotel and motor inn field. Traveling with the chains, as a rule, offers several advantages. Most of the chains, whether they be referral chains, franchise chains, self owned or operated chains, etc., have certain minimum standards and location requirements. Another advantage offered by the chains is free reservation service. Using collect phones, WATS line phones, teletypes and various electronic systems immediate confirmations of reservations are possible. A local phone call or visit to a local inn that is a member of a chain will save you the cost of a long distance call. Still another benefit is the free travel guides issued by most of these chains describing rooms, locations, and prices. These can be picked up at the local inn or will be sent upon written request. It is strongly suggested that you have these in your possession before planning your trip. Listed below are the names and addresses of most of the major chains that have these travel guides. There probably are others, however, the enclosed list is a fully adequate starting point. To avoid influencing you with the author's preferences, these are listed alphabetically:

Best Western Motels
  2910 Sky Harbor Blvd.
  Phoenix, Arizona 85034
Downtowner Motels
  202 Union Ave.
  Memphis, Tenn. 38103
Dutch Inns of America Inc.
  4685 Ponce De Leon Blvd.
  P.O. Box 1159
  Coral Gables, Fla. 33146
This is a conglomerate of Dutch Inns, American Mote-Lodge, Congress Inns, and Emmons Walker-Best Eastern.
  Holiday Inns of America
  3736 Lamar
  Memphis, Tenn. 38118
Howard Johnsons
  95-25 Queens Blvd.
  Rego Park, L.I., N.Y. 11374
Master Hosts
  6902 Freeway
  Fort Worth, Texas 76116
Quality Courts Motel Inc.
  Daytona Beach, Fla. 32015
Ramada Inns
  P.O. Box 590
  Phoenix, Arizona 85001
Sheraton Corp. of America
  470 Atlantic Ave.
  Boston, Mass. 02210
Statler Hilton
  9990 Santa Monica Blvd.
  Beverly HILLS, Calif. 90212
TraveLodge Motels
  P.O. Box 308
  El Cajon, Calif. 92022

Other chains that will make reservations for you and may or may not issue travel guides are Albert Pick, Imperial, Knott, Loews, and Titan.

One tip on all hotel reservations. If there is a possibility of arrival after 6:00 P.M., guarantee your reservation. No hotel or motel is obligated to hold a room after 6:00 P.M. if the reservation is not guaranteed.

Armed with the above information and a reasonable amount of analysis, planning and imagination, you should have no difficulty in working out the most practical and effective itineraries for your particular mode of sale.

10

RECAP

The Sale

As mentioned in the first chapter of this book, every-one is constantly selling in the normal course of events. However, we are primarily concerned with selling and salesmanship from the professional salesman's viewpoint. The professional salesman has developed the ability and the techniques of salesmanship to a point that insures his success. He knows all of the steps necessary to close his sale. His background work and research work are properly executed and he reaps the rewards of his labors.

In this book, most of the information was geared to, and aimed at the true "pro" salesman. Many retail clerks will read this volume and jump to the conclusion that the greater part of the information imparted does not apply to them. Majority of those who assume that attitude will continue to draw the limited incomes of the retail clerks and never achieve the steps up into the broader horizons. This information actually applies to anyone who would make selling a career. The only variations are in applications.

In simple form, we will repeat the steps of the sale at this point. Again the point is stressed that all of these steps are necessary to some degree. The degree will vary with product or service, price, line, customer, company, etc. The final decision of how much effort goes into each step must be left to the intelligence and discretion of the salesman.

1. Prospecting. This is the first step and refers to the exploring of potential markets to find the prospective customer to approach.

2. Approach. This is the confrontation between the salesman and the prospect in preparation for making the presentation.

3. Presentation. This is the meat of the sale. It is the telling the prospect just what you have to offer him and showing him all of the ways your proposition will benefit him.

4. Handling objections. This is actually a digression from the presentation. It consists of removing any negatives from the prospect's thoughts to establish a close.

5. Close. This is the salesman's raison d'etre. It is the asking for the contract or money and converts the prospect into a customer and keeps the home office working.

To properly execute these above outlined steps, the salesman should have a thorough knowledge of them. In addition, a good sales personality is necessary and can be developed. When all of these facets have been mastered, a good salesman is the resultant product. With this product, higher earnings, recognition, and promotions form an accompanying chorus.

Salesmanship As A Career

Salesmanship is a field unique unto itself. Unlike engineering, or accounting, etc., it cannot properly be referred to as a discipline. In no other high level aspect of business does a man have the opportunity to use his own judgement, planning and modus operandi. The proper use of one's talent, ability and training can bring outstanding rewards.

Studies of charts put out by employment agencies and studies of help wanted ads that indicate salary levels will show that sales and marketing, almost always, fall in the top 10% to 20% of remuneration in professional placement.

A continuing check of promotions to top management of corporate entities will also indicate a much greater proportion of promotions from sales and marketing than from finance or production.

Obviously, the potentials offered by a selling career are the greatest. That is they are the greatest for the man who excels in this field. You can be that man. The doors are always open.

INDEX